I0460480

Your words are worthy.
Your voice is important.

PUBLISH HER™

PUBLISH HER SOFTCOVER JOURNAL

Printed in the United States of America

Published by Publish Her, LLC
6726 Walker Street
St. Louis Park, MN 55426
www.publishherpress.com

Publish Her is a female-founded publisher dedicated to educating authors and elevating the words, stories and writing of women.

PUBLISH HER™

www.ingramcontent.com/pod-product-compliance
Lightning Source LLC
Chambersburg PA
CBHW061701120626
46550CB00003B/1040
* 9 7 9 8 9 8 8 3 4 4 4 5 2 *